Wheels Around Connaught

by
Cyril McIntyre

The Galway General Omnibus Company vehicle heading for Salthill is a Morris-Commercial (IM 1834) with 20-seat body by Fahy Brothers. The absence of any other traffic in this view of William Street is characteristic of the early days of bus operation in Galway.

© Cyril McIntyre 2004
First published in the United Kingdom, 2004,
by Stenlake Publishing Ltd.
Telephone: 01290 551122
Printed by Cordfall Ltd., Glasgow, G21 2QA

ISBN 1 84033 297 2

On Saturday 8 August 1936 the Galway General Omnibus Company was acquired by the Great Southern Railways. Ten vehicles were taken over – three Lancias, three Commers, two Bedfords, a Karrier and an Associated Daimler. This picture shows nine of these on the morning of the take-over, lined up on the north side of Eyre Square. Destination signs in Irish were in use from about 1935 on bus routes from Galway to the Irish-speaking areas of the county, long before they were adopted nationally by CIE in 1966. In its later years, the Galway General showed its name in Irish – *Bus-Chomhlucht na Gaillimhe Teoranta* – using Gaelic lettering on the bus sides accompanied by a handsome crest incorporating the city arms. *(Fahy Bros. Coachbuilders)*

FOREWORD

In Celtic times Ireland was traditionally divided into the four provinces of Ulster, Munster, Leinster and Connaught, referred to by many writers as Ireland's 'four green fields'. Connaught – the most westerly province – comprises the counties of Galway, Mayo, Sligo, Leitrim and Roscommon. The area has always had a lower density of population than the rest of the country, with a variety of rugged coastal and mountain scenery which attracted visitors even before the dawning of the age of the railways.

This selection of photographs attempts to convey an impression of the varied forms of wheeled transport which could be found around the counties of Connaught over the past two centuries, with an obvious bias towards my own personal interest in road passenger transport. In the case of photographs other than my own, I have sought permission for publication and credited the original photographers where they are known. However, a number of pictures in my collection carry no copyright information. Some of these are old picture postcards, while others have been handed down from former bus companies or vehicle builders which have long since passed into history.

Little is known about the origin and history of this Leyland charabanc (IK 2719). Its Dublin registration would suggest that it initially ran in that area just before the First World War, and it may have been sold to an operator in County Galway afterwards.

TOURIST CAR. CLIFDEN. Co.GALWAY. 4309. W.L.

For many years prior to the First World War the only form of public transport in numerous rural areas of Ireland was the mail car. Most of these had their origins in the network of public car services inaugurated by Charles Bianconi, an Italian immigrant who ran his first vehicle between Clonmel and Cahir in 1815. By 1845 Bianconi had cars running to all the principal towns in the West of Ireland. With the growth of the railways the importance of the car services declined, except in the more remote areas not served by rail. In 1867 Bianconi sold all his car routes, in most cases to his local agents and managers, and retired from business. This County Galway scene at Mullarkey's Hotel in Clifden is typical of travel in Connaught before the advent of motorised transport. (*National Library of Ireland*)

A lone motorist skirts the shores of Lough Corrib in the early years of the twentieth century. In those pioneering days of motor transport, road surfaces, designed to cater for horse-drawn carts, were very primitive and posed a constant threat of damage to the tyres and springs of equally primitive cars and charabancs. Repairs were entrusted by the county councils to local road contractors, who struggled to cope with the increasing wear and tear caused by heavier and faster mechanically propelled vehicles. It has not been possible to determine the make of the car, but the English registration (H 6519) suggests it was driven either by a wealthy tourist in search of 'hunting, shooting and fishing', or perhaps by an official of the Congested Districts' Board on a tour of inspection! The latter was established by the British government in 1891 to develop agriculture and industry in the counties along the western seaboard. *(National Library of Ireland)*

The Mall and Railway Hotel, Westport.

From 1911 the Midland Great Western Railway operated a car service between Clifden railway station and Westport (see front cover caption), where the terminus was at the Railway Hotel on the tree-lined Mall, overlooking the Carrabeg River. A contemporary guidebook praised the town as 'well built', adding that 'its clean and wide streets are lighted with gas, and it possesses a good water supply'. The gates at the end of the Mall led to the demesne of Westport House, home of the Marquis of Sligo, described as 'a sweet sylvan retreat, to which the inhabitants of the neighbourhood have free access'. The car route ran from Clifden to Leenane, continuing to Westport either via Louisburgh or inland via the Erriff Valley. Operations ceased after the 1916 season and the cars were sold in 1918.

RAILWAY STATION. ACHILL. 5086. W.L.

In 1894 the MGWR opened a branch line from Westport to Mallaranny. The following year this was extended to Achill Sound, where the journey to Achill Island could be completed across an iron swivel bridge. It was one of a number of lines built with government funding under legislation of 1889. These became known as the Balfour lines, after the Chief Secretary for Ireland who proposed the legislation. This view of the Achill terminus features a typical MGWR local train, headed by locomotive 110, *Bat*. In common with many similar branch lines throughout rural Ireland it never attracted large volumes of either passenger or goods traffic and was closed on 31 December 1934. It reopened from April 1936 to facilitate reconstruction of the roads in the area, and finally closed on 30 September 1937. (*National Library of Ireland*)

At Galway, the Midland Great Western Railway built the first of its three hotels, with convenient access by a private walkway at the end of the station platforms. The station opened in August 1851 and despite modernisation is largely unaltered from its original structure. The carriages in this view, dating from 1877, are typical of the standard six-wheel design favoured by many of the Irish railway companies up to the early years of the twentieth century. *(National Library of Ireland)*

For almost 40 years the popular seaside resort of Salthill, a little over two miles west of Galway, enjoyed the distinction of being the most westerly tram terminus in Europe. The Galway & Salthill Tramway, opened on 1 October 1879, was a single track line with a number of passing loops, built to the narrow gauge of three feet. Two types of four-wheel trams were operated. There were five open-top double deckers, drawn by two horses and carrying 36 passengers. For winter use two covered one-horse single deckers were placed in service in 1888. Services ran every twenty minutes during the summer and every half hour during the winter months. Here heavily laden double decker No. 2, en route from Salthill to Eyre Square, is unobstructed by any other wheeled traffic! *(National Library of Ireland)*

Within months of the closure of the tramway a group of local business-people formed the Galway General Omnibus Company to restore the public transport link between Galway and Salthill using motor buses. One of its earliest vehicles was an open-top Commer double decker placed in service in August 1919. This was replaced in May 1924 by a Karrier open-top double decker with 49 seats (IM 1815), which operated until at least 1929 and is believed to have been withdrawn as a result of a fatal accident involving a passenger falling from the upper deck. More typical of the Galway General fleet is this Lancia dating from 1926 (IM 2634), with 26-seat bodywork by local coachbuilder Fahy Brothers of Forster Street, off Eyre Square. There is little other traffic to be seen at the Salthill bus terminus, while beyond the wide expanse of Galway Bay sweeps out to sea and the distant coastline of County Clare.

Below: A view of Salthill showing a solitary bus en route to the city approaching a delivery dray heading in the opposite direction – probably with parcels from the railway station for some of the many hotels and guest houses in the area.

Opposite: The tramline started in Eyre Square, the heart of Galway and convenient to the railway station and several major hotels. This view, again of tram No. 2, dates from the closing years of the nineteenth century and conveys the busy atmosphere of market day, with a variety of carts and drays competing for road space. The Bank of Ireland dominates the north side of the square, its architecture contrasting with Burke's 'Posting Establishment' (with its two dormer windows) and the adjoining office of the *Galway Pilot* newspaper, which for some years was used by the Irish Omnibus Company as its office and bus terminus. A horse-drawn bus waits outside the Imperial and Royal Hotels, beside which traditional thatched cottages can also be seen. Labour troubles and difficulties caused by the First World War resulted in the closure of the tramway in January 1919. (*National Library of Ireland*)

SALTHILL AND GALWAY BAY, GALWAY.

This view of William Street, Galway, shows the horse-drawn float used for delivering parcels from the railway station, liveried with the CIE crest in light green on a dark green background. The buildings have changed little since the days of the Galway General bus illustrated on page 1. Dillon's jewellery shop is still selling Claddagh rings and the clock on the shop wall still proclaims 'Dublin Time' to local shoppers and visiting tourists. The car parked by the kerbside is a pre-war Ford model Y, known commonly throughout Ireland as the 'baby' Ford.

Street, Clifden Co. Galway.

4393

By the mid-1930s the hotel in Clifden's Main Street had become the Clifden Bay Hotel (it appears as the Railway Hotel in the picture on the inside front cover), and cars were more plentiful in the town. Careful inspection of the picture reveals that the conductor is busy loading luggage on to the roof carrier of a Leyland Badger belonging to the Great Southern Railways. A Leyland lorry of the GSR road freight department is just visible at the far end of the street.

GSR 506 at Leenane on 17 July 1934, en route from Westport to Clifden. This was one of a batch of fifteen vehicles put in service by the Irish Omnibus Company in 1930, and was a Leyland Badger goods chassis fitted with a 20-seater bus body. The fifteen buses were used on rural routes where the volume of business was low or where road conditions were unsuitable for the standard 32-seater buses. When the railway line between Galway and Clifden was closed on 20 April 1935, Leyland Badgers were also used on the substitute bus route until the roads were brought up to the standard needed to permit the operation of larger vehicles. In 1937 all the Badgers were withdrawn and converted to lorries for the GSR road freight department.

A number of them survived to become part of the CIE fleet in 1945. (*H. C. Casserley*)

As well as building bus bodies for the Galway General Omnibus Company and other local bus operators, the coachbuilding firm of Fahy Brothers turned out a wide variety of specialist vehicles at their works in Forster Street. Hearses were built for undertakers throughout the country, and this example on a Ford V8 chassis was supplied in 1938 to Terence O'Connor & Sons of Shandon Street, Cork. *(Fahy Bros. Coachbuilders)*

Another Fahy speciality sought by customers such as estate owners, hackney operators and mail car contractors was the 'station wagon' conversion based on the Fordson half-ton van chassis. This example was photographed immediately after completion but before registration outside a local Ford dealer's premises. *(Fahy Bros. Coachbuilders)*

The GBC bakery, confectionery shop and restaurant in Galway's Williamsgate Street is a long-established local business and still thriving today. In 1935 it acquired this fine Bedford van (IM 4679) with Fahy bodywork for express deliveries of bread and cakes to customers throughout the city and county. *(Fahy Bros. Coachbuilders)*

Galway has long been noted for its annual racing festival which takes place every year during the last week of July. This Leyland Tiger horse box operated by the Great Northern Railway and based at Dundalk was a regular sight at Galway races for several years. Originally built in 1930 as a bus (No. 97, ZI 4280) with 31-seat body by the City Wheel Works (Dublin), it was rebuilt as a four-horse box in 1945 and operated in this form until 1954.

16

Poor road conditions again resulted in the use of non-standard small buses at the Galway depot in 1951, this time on the route to Lettermullen. Galway County Council imposed weight restrictions on the bridges at Annaghvane and Bealadangan and the normal service buses were replaced by Bedford 25-seat coaches. Six of these vehicles were built in 1948 by Griffith J. Roberts of Grangegorman in Dublin on Bedford OB chassis. Originally ordered by Blue Cars Continental of London for the operation of Irish tours, they were bought by CIE in 1949 and used initially on the special service between the city air terminal and Dublin Airport. By 1951 this service required larger vehicles and the Bedfords were transferred to Galway. BP 1 is pictured near Carraroe. *(R. Marshall)*

The condition of the bridges on the Lettermullen route was so bad that, even using the lighter Bedford vehicles, passengers had to alight from the buses and follow them across on foot, as instructed by a large bilingual notice in the saloon. Other unusual features in the Bedfords, known as *busóga* by local passengers, included a sliding sun roof, interior mirrors and a clock. One vehicle (BP 6), seen here at Galway railway station on 22 August 1953, was painted in the CIE coach livery of light green with a dark green stripe and gold crest for use on summer season day tours of Connemara.

17

In contrast to the high-frequency Salthill route from Galway which was supplemented by every available spare bus on fine summer days, the route from Renmore to Taylor's Hill ran only every 50 minutes and required just one vehicle to maintain the service throughout the day. For many years that bus was T 4, a Leyland Tiger built in 1935, seen here in Galway's Eglinton Street in August 1951. Formerly GSR 484, it was one of only eight diesel-engined single deckers which passed to CIE in 1945 and lasted in service until 1960. *(Copyright Alan B. Cross)*

Seen on that same sunny day in August 1951 as T 4 (facing page), but working on the Salthill route, is NP 26 (formerly GSR 762), a Leyland Lion 32-seater dating from 1936. *(Copyright Alan B. Cross)*

Despite its imposing title, the Sligo, Leitrim & Northern Counties Railway had just one cross-country line from Enniskillen in County Fermanagh to Collooney in County Sligo. From there, trains completed the journey to Sligo on the CIE line. The company also ran a small bus fleet on local routes from Blacklion and Manorhamilton to Sligo, including some buses acquired second-hand from the Great Northern Railway. This is a Gardner-engined bus, built at the GNR Dundalk works in 1937, pictured at Eyre Square in Galway on a football special on Sunday 14 July 1957.

A mixture of traffic on Williamsgate Street near the junction with Eyre Square in the summer of 1956. The Ransomes mobile crane is returning to the CIE freight depot at the railway station after completing the task of unloading crates of machinery from a railhead delivery lorry at a merchant's premises in the city.

For many years delivery of parcels and light goods from railway stations all over Ireland was carried out using horse-drawn transport, but in the mid-1960s CIE gradually replaced the horses with mechanised vehicles. Just as the ubiquitous Ford tractor replaced horses on the farms, so it also displaced horse-power for railhead delivery work, hauling specially built drawbar trailers with a carrying capacity of about two tons. CIE had a few hundred of these tractors, some of which are seen at Galway goods depot on a quiet Sunday afternoon in August 1968.

By 1968 CIE single decker buses were sporting a new red and cream livery, evoking memories for some people of the red and white IOC and GSR buses of the thirties. Even the destination signs for places outside the Gaeltacht areas were displayed in Irish by this time. On 10 July 1968, P 195, a Leyland Tiger built in 1949 with CIE 39-seat body, waits to leave from Eyre Square for *Bóthar na Trá* (Salthill), following the same route as that of the Galway General buses over 40 years earlier.

Galway had a distinctive local variation of the CIE blue and cream livery applied to double deckers from 1961 onwards, with an additional blue band between the upper and lower decks. Photographed at Eglinton Street en route from Taylor's Hill to Renmore is R 435, a Leyland Titan dating from 1949, one of a fleet of 150 double deckers supplied complete by Leyland Motors to CIE to replace the last of Dublin's trams and expand the bus network to serve new housing areas.

Development of long-distance express coach services in Ireland was hindered by a policy which treated bus services as subordinate to the railway network, but from 1961 onwards a number of express routes were introduced to replace closed railway lines. A major development in 1967 was the commencement of a service between Galway and Belfast jointly operated by CIE and Ulsterbus. This Ulsterbus Leyland Leopard was photographed at Galway railway station on 10 July 1968 after an evening arrival from Belfast. The first generation of Ulsterbus express coaches carried the brand name Wolfhound Express.

The tourism boom of the 1960s saw a big increase in the number of independent coach companies providing coaches on contract to incoming tour operators – principally those catering for the lucrative American market. Seen outside the Imperial Hotel on Eyre Square is a Bedford coach bodied by Duffy Coachbuilders of Dundalk and operated by O'Grady Coach Tours of Dublin.

Photographed at Cong Pier on Lough Corrib in May 1970, passengers on a CIE tour board their coach after travelling from Galway on the Corrib lake cruiser *Maid of Coleraine*. The coach is a Leyland Worldmaster built at the CIE Spa Road works in 1963. Its futuristic body was designed by David Ogle Design of Letchworth, whose work included such diverse vehicles as the Reliant Robin three-wheeler car and the Leyland Popemobile used during the papal visit to Britain in 1982.

CIE was among the first railways in Europe to eliminate steam motive power. The first stage of railway dieselisation involved the introduction in 1952 of a fleet of diesel railcars for main line passenger services. Built by Park Royal Vehicles of Middlesex and incorporating AEC bus-type engines mounted underneath the carriage floors, they ushered in a new era of comfort and speed on the Irish railways. Here a Dublin-bound express waits at Galway station on a summer Sunday evening in 1968. The CIE area headquarters building is in the background.

Pearse Street, Ballina, *c*.1928, showing an Associated Daimler bus belonging to the Magnet Bus Company which started the first service on the Dublin to Ballina route on 18 May 1927. With several large signs on the front, potential passengers were left in no doubt about where the service was going! Another bus is just visible behind the Ford Model T car parked on the left, while the poor road surface is typical of that found in many Irish towns at the time.

Knox Street, Ballina.

Another postcard view of Ballina, this time showing Knox Street with a Leyland Lion of the Irish Omnibus Company to the fore. The IOC and the Magnet Bus Company competed vigorously on the routes linking Ballina and Westport with Dublin, especially in their efforts to carry the migrant harvesters who travelled from all over the western counties in search of seasonal work in Britain. In 1929 the IOC became a subsidiary of the Great Southern Railways and bought out Magnet in 1932.

Even before the closure of the Achill branch railway line, both Magnet and IOC buses were running right across Achill Island to Keel and Dooagh. This 1954 view depicts a standard CIE Leyland Tiger (eight feet wide) en route to Dooagh from Westport.

Taken close to the same location as the previous picture, but proceeding in the opposite direction (to Westport), Leyland Tiger P 305 was one of a batch of narrower (7' 6") vehicles which were allocated mainly to depots in the western counties. Both the driver and conductor are busy loading and sorting suitcases on the roof luggage carrier, which was a feature of most Irish country buses until the advent of driver-only operation from 1961 onwards. (*The Omnibus Society – John F. Parke Collection*)

The religious shrine at the Mayo village of Knock, seven miles from Claremorris, attracts thousands of pilgrims, especially on Sundays, from all parts of the country. Before the growth in levels of car ownership, large numbers of visitors travelled on special pilgrimage trains to Claremorris, completing the journey to Knock Shrine by bus. CIE provided ambulance transport for invalid pilgrims using both converted buses and purpose-built vehicles. In May 1951 the company purchased two Ford ambulances for this work, seen here at Broadstone works in Dublin before moving to their operational base at Ballina bus garage. *(CIE)*

In later years larger vehicles were needed to cope with the transport requirements of invalids and converted buses were used exclusively. The ambulance fleet based at Ballina in 1970 comprised four Gardner-engined buses originally built in 1950 by the Great Northern Railway and converted in 1964 to carry eight stretchers each. G 387 is pictured at the bus park near the church at Knock.

Moving the pilgrims to and from the trains at Claremorris every Sunday required the use of every available bus from the garages at Ballina, Sligo and Galway. Many of these buses operated special pilgrimage services from their home depots before taking up the railway shuttle service, and buses bringing pilgrimage groups from other parts of the country would also be pressed into service. E 127 is one of a fleet of 170 similar Leyland Leopards placed in service by CIE between 1961 and 1964; these were the last single deckers to be built at the Spa Road CIE works with the traditional roof luggage carrier.

The Knock Shrine ambulances were not the only unusual passenger vehicles in the CIE fleet during the 1950s, and it also included a number of Ford station wagons operated in connection with the Great Southern Hotels, usually for ferrying guests and staff to and from the nearest railway station. In 1953, ZH 597 was based at the Great Southern Hotel in Mallaranny. The Chrysler saloon parked beside it is typical of those used at the time by limousine operators, including CIE, for small parties of wealthy American tourists. *(CIE)*

O'CONNELL STREET, SLIGO.

R.668

Quieter days in O'Connell Street, Sligo, with only a solitary car on the move and no shortage of parking spaces in this 1930s view. The bus, waiting to depart for Strandhill, was one of a number operated by John Carew, who also owned the Swan Hotel and Ballroom at the popular seaside resort. Carew's service to Strandhill was taken over by the Great Southern Railways in May 1940.

Sligo's other seaside resort, Rosses Point, was served for many years by two independent bus operators from the same family – Patrick and Margaret Gillan. Both sold out to the Great Southern Railways in September 1937. The GSR acquired EI 2986, a 20-seat Commer Centaur, from Patrick Gillan. After a short period in GSR service it was sold in February 1941 to the Irish Red Cross for use as a mobile canteen, and was photographed in the Dundrum area of Dublin in August 1951. (*Copyright Alan B. Cross*)

The Sligo, Leitrim & Northern Counties Railway followed the example of other Irish railway companies in pioneering the use of diesel traction in an effort to cut running costs. Early experiments by the Great Northern Railway involved fitting railway wheels to a conventional road bus to create an uniquely Irish vehicle – the 'railbus' – which could also tow a trailer for carrying luggage and parcels. As well as the rear boarding platform at normal height, there were steps down to ground level, so that passengers could be picked up at road crossings and other convenient locations which lacked platforms. This Associated Daimler railbus of the SL&NCR was formerly a road bus in the Great Northern Railway fleet. In due course it was replaced by another former GNR vehicle bearing the same fleet number – this time an AEC Reliance bus which gained an extended lease of life as a rail vehicle.

Shortly after the formation of CIE in 1945, the company acquired over 200 AEC Matador lorries to replace a variety of over-age freight vehicles inherited from the Great Southern Railways. This bulk grain container was an early CIE experiment in demountable bodies to fit the Matador chassis, which could also carry furniture lift vans and livestock containers. This type of 'lift-on, lift-off' operation increased the flexibility of the road freight fleet and enabled CIE to cater for various specialised goods movements with seasonal fluctuations in demand. The grain units frequently worked in the Sligo area serving the Pollexfen mills. *(CIE)*

At Sligo railway station in 1951, the Saturdays-only service to Maugherow was worked by NP 58, a Leyland Lion 32-seater of the former Great Southern Railways fleet, built in 1939. *(Copyright Alan B. Cross)*

The Great Northern Railway, which operated bus services north of Sligo and through County Donegal to Derry, had a separate Sligo terminus and office in Quay Street. Here the company's first post-war double decker, an AEC Regent with Park Royal bodywork, waits to depart on a service to Donegal town. Although displaying 'Donegal' on the destination indicator, a low railway bridge at Laghey precluded the operation of double deckers beyond that point. Normal practice was for the double decker to operate as far as Ballyshannon, where passengers for Donegal and Derry transferred to a single decker to continue the journey northwards. *(The Omnibus Society – John F. Parke Collection)*

After the acquisition of the Great Northern bus services by CIE in 1958, the GNR office in Quay Street was closed and the railway station at Sligo became the terminus for all bus services. The square, almost utility appearance of a Leyland Leopard (E 118) built in 1964 contrasts with the more streamlined shape of the Park Royal bodywork on a former Great Northern AEC Regal (AU 344) dating from 1955. From 1961 onwards driver-only operation of CIE provincial services became widespread and former GNR vehicles were converted to front-entrance layout to facilitate this development.

(Robert L. Grieves)

Further contrasting styles at Sligo railway station – Leyland Leopard E 120 is on the former GNR route to Ballyshannon, while the local service to Rosses Point is worked by Leyland Tiger P 148 dating from 1949. The continuing conversion of rural routes to driver-only operation hastened the withdrawal of the P-type Leyland Tigers, but many of them saw extended service as school buses from 1967 onwards following the introduction of a nationwide school transport scheme. *(Robert L. Grieves)*

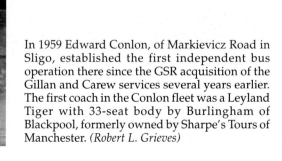

In 1959 Edward Conlon, of Markievicz Road in Sligo, established the first independent bus operation there since the GSR acquisition of the Gillan and Carew services several years earlier. The first coach in the Conlon fleet was a Leyland Tiger with 33-seat body by Burlingham of Blackpool, formerly owned by Sharpe's Tours of Manchester. *(Robert L. Grieves)*

The bus services of the Sligo, Leitrim & Northern Counties Railway originated with the takeover in 1945 of the route between Blacklion and Sligo operated by Appleby's Bus Service of Enniskillen. Three years later saw the arrival of the only buses bought new by the SL&NCR – both were Commer Commando types with 32-seater bodies by Browne Coachbuilders of Sligo. One is seen here at Manorhamilton on 8 June 1953, with a freight lorry just visible behind it. After the railway closed in September 1957 these buses were bought by the International Express Company of Bundoran.

(John C. Gillham)

The village of Carrigallen in County Leitrim had had its own local bus service since the early 1930s, and from 1938 onwards this became part of the Erne Bus Service based in Enniskillen. In 1957, when the Enniskillen operator was acquired by the Ulster Transport Authority, the Carrigallen services were sold to Edward Maguire, the Erne driver based in Carrigallen. He continued to operate using the Erne Bus Service name for many years. The fleet included some Leyland Tigers bought second-hand from the Ulster Transport Authority – MZ 352 was built in 1948 for the Northern Ireland Road Transport Board and was bought by Maguire in 1964. *(Copyright Alan B. Cross)*

The narrow gauge Cavan & Leitrim Railway, opened on 17 October 1887, provided a link from Dromod – on the Midland Great Western Railway's line from Dublin to Sligo – to Belturbet on the Great Northern Railway network. The following year, on 2 May 1888, a branch was opened from the mid-point of the line at Ballinamore to Arigna to serve the collieries of the Arigna Valley. Amalgamated into the Great Southern Railways in 1925, the line never enjoyed any degree of prosperity and closure came on 31 March 1959. This view of Locomotive No. 1 (renumbered 1L by the GSR) in the dying days of CIE operation of the line also shows the unroofed cattle wagons typical of many Irish narrow gauge lines. *(P. Flanagan)*

Magnet Bus leaving Post Office, Athlone.

Athlone has long been regarded as a gateway to Connaught, and because of its position straddling the River Shannon became a natural junction of both rail and road routes to and from all parts of Ireland. Although most of Athlone is in County Westmeath, part of the town is on the County Roscommon side of the Shannon and hence geographically in Connaught. The first bus service between Athlone and Dublin was run by Gordon's Motor Service of Cavan, trading as 'Magnet' and commencing on 25 October 1926. Here a Reo 20-seater prepares to leave for Dublin from the post office, possibly on the inaugural trip judging from the number of onlookers waiting to watch it depart.

CHURCH STREET, ATHLONE.

The success of the Magnet service between Athlone and Dublin attracted a rival service run by the Irish Omnibus Company, which commenced in July 1927. Many of the IOC routes were operated under contract on behalf of the Great Southern Railways. Here an IOC Leyland Lion is seen in Church Street en route for Dublin.